CUSSING for KIDS!

Etiquette for the Profane

Jimmy Huston

Cosworth Publishing
21545 Yucatan Avenue
Woodland Hills CA 91364
www.cosworthpublishing.com

For information regarding permission,
please send an email to office@cosworthpublishing.com.

This book is dedicated to all the dear friends and family members who have asked not to be named.

Preface

There are no cuss words in this book.

You already know them all anyway — what's the point?

This book is about how to cuss, how to cuss well, when to cuss, and how to get away with it. There's also a bit about where to cuss.

That's enough.

So, there will be no cuss words in this book.

Unless I get mad.

Why Do We Cuss?

Because we have to.

With life, comes trouble. Things never go as well as they should, and cussing offers a quick pick-me-up, an energizing cheap thrill, or a generic substitute for knowing the right thing to say.

Cussing is one of the spices of life. Even when life is good, cussing can make it better. It adds emphasis. And, it is oddly inclusive — cussing works best when there's an audience. Cussing is an ancient form of public discourse. It provides a universal rating system of how you're really feeling about things.

Usually no one really teaches us how to cuss. We have to pick it up "in the streets," and perhaps that is as it should be. Imagine how colorless cussing would be if it was presented from the front of the classroom or a courtroom or a place of worship. If the authority figures and role models in our lives "approved" of cussing, what would be the point? Screw 'em. (See how it works?)

That's probably why there are no college courses in cussing, and no post-graduate degrees or honors, like *magna cum profanity*. Perhaps in some dark future these pages can become a textbook on the subject. In the meantime, hopefully, this modest book will provide a bit of guidance, ranging from surly nuance to simply being gross.

One quick note on an age-old academic question. Is it "cussing" or "cursing?" Yes.

It is both. One is correct. The other is right. Obviously, use "cursing" if you're a stiff and you think you're too good to use "cussing." Otherwise, use "cussing." "Cursing" would be an entirely different book.

Busted!

You've been caught, right? That's why you're reading this book — you've gotten yourself in trouble for cussing. (If you haven't, you will.)

So what's the big deal? Maybe you just wanted to be bad for a change, without doing anything *really* bad. Cussing is certainly better than armed robbery, murder, or being a politician.

Cussing is powerful. It can make you feel good. It can also make you pretty low afterwards if you've chosen the wrong time, place, person, or wording — so be careful. Before you cut loose with heated words, look around. Who's watching? Who's listening? Who's got a cell phone pointed at you?

If you're going to cuss, don't whine about getting caught. That's the deal.

Getting caught is just another way of saying, "Someone's listening," but if no one is listening, what's the point of cussing anyway?

How do you get away with it?

Be smart. Be subtle. Be devious. And, be ready to apologize (without any more cussing). Pretend that you've learned your lesson.

Say that it just slipped out. Yeah, that's a good one. Try that. It was an accident in the heat of the moment. Good luck.

At Home

All homes are different. Some have absolutely no cussing. Others have lots and lots of cussing.

Mom and Dad may cuss, but that doesn't necessarily mean they want *you* to cuss. Some kids have parents who would never cuss, especially not in front of them.

You can safely assume that if Mom and Dad don't cuss, they certainly don't want you to.

On the other hand, if your answer to, "Where did you learn those filthy words?" is, "From Mom," then you're pretty much off the hook. Cuss away!

Cussing Well

Some people may think that it's bad for you to cuss, but they will think even less of you if you cuss poorly.

If you're cussing, you certainly don't want to sound like an amateur. You may be using words that you *think* you know the meaning of — but you're not absolutely certain. Find out. You don't want to be shouting things that make you look stupid. So make sure you're using the words properly. Look them up.

Some cuss words are wildly versatile, but stay on track. There may be acceptable variations and there may be ideas that are new to you. Be open to them.

Really good cussing requires an excellent and colorful vocabulary, accented by performance. That means speaking clearly, perhaps at high volume, while demonstrating sincerity, mood, clarity, and suitably unclean thoughts.

Remember, there's nothing worse than getting in trouble for cussing and then having an authority figure tell your parents that you weren't even doing it right.

Body parts

It all starts with the simple names of our body parts. They vary a little from person to person, and even more from gender to gender, but we all have them, so it's no big deal.

For some reason, however, we're not supposed to talk about them, except perhaps in the bathroom, the locker room, or the doctor's office.

There are already perfectly good words to refer to body parts, but those words usually seem stuffy and they're certainly no fun. There are other names we use — better names — that will make people laugh. You already know what they are. Some of those names have become actual cuss words. And, that's why we love 'em. Nobody wants to use medical nomenclature when cussing will do. It's just biology. Enjoy.

Also, some people consider it impolite to refer to body parts in the presence of the opposite sex. Not true. They will be delighted.

As the years go by, it all gets considerably more complicated, so you'll want to be prepared. Start early.

Bodily Functions

They're perfectly normal, at least most of the time, but some body parts have a tendency to leak, and sometimes things just come shooting out. This happens to everybody, but we're not really supposed to talk about it. Maybe it's because of the smell.

There are lots of names for the silly things that come out of us. These names are usually considered a form of cussing (if you do it right), especially if you're in school or church. Be careful when you use them. They may be wet.

Showing Off

This is what's behind most cussing.

Before you blast off, you probably should consider your audience.

Maybe you really do want to show off to your teacher.

Maybe you do want your parents to see and hear how you feel about something, and you're ready to take the heat.

Or, maybe you just want to impress your friends.

First, be sure that these are the friends you really want. If they're that easy to impress, they may not be making the best judgements themselves.

And, it may get harder to make new friends once you've shown everyone your louder, darker side. Just a thought.

The downside of showing off is that your audience is adjusting their opinions of you and it can be hard to win them back.

Most adults will cut you some slack. They've seen and heard worse. But, you never know what's coming in life, and the day may come when you'll want them to have a kind opinion of you for some reason.

Don't embarrass yourself in front of someone who's going to be important to you. It's really hard to get un-embarrassed.

Anger

The madder you are, the bigger you cuss. That's the way it works.

If you're mad enough, you don't even have to be right. Just keep cussing. And more cussing, bigger and badder. Eventually you'll have to repeat yourself, but that's okay. It's all part of it. (There are only so many good and awful words to use.)

It's called a "catharsis," and it's like vomiting words. If you're doing it right, children and small animals will run away in fear.

Frustration

Sometimes you just have to let it all out — and it probably won't all come out unless you add a little cussing.

This is a special type of cussing that may happen even when there's no one around to hear it. So what's the point? It makes you feel better. You let off some steam. You release a little stress. Maybe you even spread it around.

Of course the truth is that cussing doesn't solve your problem, whatever it is. It just feels good. But that's enough. Cuss on.

Description

When adjectives fail, or aren't quite strong enough, cussing comes in handy for extra flavor. Even when applied to simple words, a choice cuss word can spice up an uninspired description quite a bit. When cussing is applied with distinction to describe a person of import, additional heat is brought into play.

Perhaps the most delightful examples occur when a cuss word adjective describes another cuss word noun, becoming doubly offensive.

Some special cuss words can be used as almost every part of speech — certainly as a noun, verb, adjective, and adverb. Pick your favorites and see how many different ways you can use them. Instead of, "You're a blank," it becomes a much improved, "Blank you, you blankety-blanking blanker." Cussing can be educational.

Emphasis

Sometimes you just can't think of the best way to describe something. In this situation many people turn to cussing to emphasize a description, an action, a person, or whatever. Try changing your speaking level, or speaking super-slowly, or mouthing the words silently.

In certain cases, skilled cussers will repeat the same word over and over and over to great effect.

Additional emphasis can be added by lowering your voice to a demonic whisper. If you also squeeze your eyes shut and tremble, most people will back away. Chanting incessantly also works.

Solitary Cussing

If you're alone and you're cussing, something's wrong. You're hurt, or frustrated, or angry, or *really, really* angry. This is when you can get it all out.

Since there's no one to hear you, you can say whatever you like, as loudly as you like. Don't hold back. There may even be tears involved, or spittle.

Scream bloody murder if you like. But first, look around and make *absolutely* sure you're alone.

Insults

Perhaps one of the best uses of cussing is insulting people and name calling. It's a good way to add emphasis and power — but, it can make people mad. You might want to think twice because of that.

If you're still committed to an insult, remember to make it personal. Personal attacks are referred to as *ad hominem* and are considered rude and vulgar. That's the whole point.

Almost every cuss word can be used as an insult. If one doesn't quite work, just say it louder. People will know when they're being insulted, especially when there's a lot of cussing going on.

Pardon my French

Not a real excuse, but it's *so* cute — the first time you hear it.

Still, it's worth a try. You get busted with a mouth full of cuss words, give 'em your best semi-innocent smile and feign embarrassment with a whispered, "Pardon my French." It could work.

Humor

Sometimes cussing can make something funny. Usually it's because it's somehow inappropriate or really gross, but it doesn't carry all the ugliness of some other cussing. It's almost innocent.

As usual, be careful. What seems funny now may not be so funny later. It may not be funny to people around you. It may not seem funny at all after your parents hear about it.

Performance

It's not just what you say — it's how you say it.

Be theatrical. Consider your body language.

Speak clearly, don't mumble. Be emphatic. If appropriate, yell. Or scream.

Repercussions

One of the reasons for cussing is to get a reaction.

Think ahead. Make sure that the reaction you're going to get is one you can deal with.

Cops, bullies, and parents can all make you pay.

One quick comment can lead to a lot of trouble.

The Finger

This is a really "handy" way to cuss. Sometimes you
need to cuss quietly (like across a classroom), or
across a great distance (like a football stadium). Or,
even in another language.

That's when the "finger" is a perfect fit. It's frequently
used in traffic, too, but has real world consquences
that can lead to "Road Rage" incidents that are quite
violent. Be careful.

The Ladies

It should go without saying (but it doesn't), that girls are no different, probably because they *are* different. All girls are expected to be "good girls," and at some point that becomes a little boring. Or they get a little mad. Or whatever.

So, as you probably already know, girls cuss, too. Sometimes it's cute. Sometimes it's horrific. Get out of their way.

Blasphemy

This is big league cussing. Blasphemy comes from religion and when you mess with people's religion, it can get ugly in a hurry.

Many people take this really seriously. And God may, too. There's some longstanding silly rule about taking his name in vain. Most of us aren't quite sure what it means to take someone's name "in vain," because it's such an odd expression. Basically, it means cussing, in combination with various names such as "God" and "Lord," and perhaps even "Holy" or "Almighty."

So, this kind of cussing is a little more serious. It makes people think differently about what you're saying, and about you. And they'll remember it longer.

For some people, there is no way back from this. If you're going to get biblical, you're going big. Watch your step, kid.

It's one thing to make your teacher mad. It's another thing entirely to anger God.

Slang

Sometimes circumstances (or cowardice) create a situation where cussing — even for sworn advocates — is too much. In these cases, bad language can be substituted with semi-bad language. Slang provides a rich tapestry of semi-cusswords that reflect the speaker's actual intent, but skirt the letter of the law.

The slang words of choice are the ones that have a clear antecedent, so that the intent of the semi-cuss is clear. Words such as dang, darn, heck, gosh, and others are pale imitators of their origins, but when prudence requires, they will do. It is, perhaps, the difference between getting a good scolding or a far less desirable walloping. The choice is yours, and there is no disgrace in the occasional choice of propriety at the expense of self-expression.

Some wimps do this all the time, and there are lots of acceptable words that offer alternatives to cussing. They're all boring.

Substitution

In addition to slang, there are people who use alternative words that aren't really even slangish. Jumping Jehosephat, for example. Or Jiminy Christmas. Holy Mackerel. Really? That's the best you've got?

Admittedly, these people lose some of the power of their language and, frankly, sound pretty lame. You can't express true outrage with puffery.

There are even people who switch cuss words with the names of flowers. Shouting "Chrysanthemum" or "Daffodil" or *"PETUNIA"* can't offer much of a release, but perhaps it will lighten the mood instead.

These people do not do well in gangs.

Mobile Cussing

The great thing about cussing someone when you're in a car — assuming they're not in the same car — is that they can't hear you.

The bad thing is that your parents are driving. They can definitely hear you. So shut up.

Your day will come. And when it does, remember this. If the person you're cussing is also in a car, he or she (or they) can follow you wherever you're going. That's not good.

Be Creative

People have been using the same old cuss words for centuries, from one country to another, and from one language to another. You can do better than that.

Find a new way. Sometimes it means combining words in new ways. Or, it can mean using an old word in a new context that amplifies its meaning.

That probably includes an *unusually* inappropriate setting — perhaps wildly inappropriate. Be careful.

Maybe delve into a new language or find a historical origin in ancient texts or statuary.

Getting Caught

Don't whine. You got caught cussing — because you were cussing. You were being tough. Suck it up.

Next time, be careful.

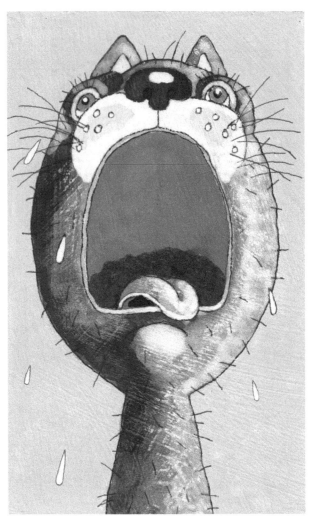

Getting Cussed At

There's a flip side to cussing — that's "getting cussed at." No matter how righteous you are in the things you shout at someone, he or she is probably going to cuss back at you. This is totally unfair, definitely uncalled for, and terribly offensive.

It proves that you were absolutely right about them.

Cussing Back

Okay, you cussed at someone, who cussed at you in return, and now you're going to cuss back. This is called "arguing," and it doesn't usually lead to much that's good.

Usually the next step is called "fighting," and it can lead to pain and other unpleasant things. Are you ready for that? Really?

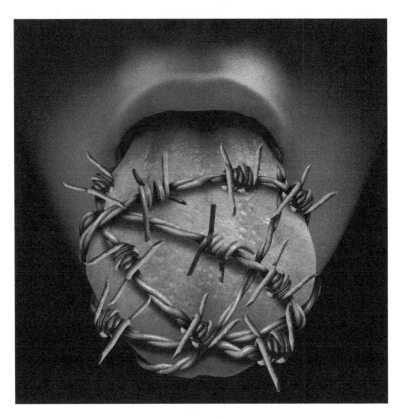

Words Hurt

In fact, that's what some of them are meant to do. But take it easy. There's a point where cussing can cross over into bullying. That's not cool. And it can lead to a severe beating from even bigger bullies.

If you can't take it, don't dish it out. The wrong kind of cussing can come back to haunt you.

As a general rule, if you make someone cry, you're both going to remember it for the rest of your lives.

Advanced Cussing

According to current U.S. laws, the topic of *Advanced Cussing* is too advanced for this book.

Watch for the sequel, ***Advanced Cussing for Kids,*** in a book store near you. Ask for it loudly. If they don't have it, feel free to demonstrate what you learned in this book with a furious and fabulous tirade.

Timing

There may or may not be a proper time to cuss, but there are definitely times *not* to cuss. When you're in the principal's office, for instance. Or, during the national anthem, or religious ceremonies: weddings, funerals, bar mitzvahs, etc. You already know all this.

Of course that's going to tempt you even more to try a little cussing when you shouldn't. You've been warned.

Censorship

Sometimes cowards interfere with the free expression of ideas, including bad language.

This issue has been taken all the way to the United States Supreme Court and they have ruled that freedom of speech always wins out! Except at your house. Your Mom and Dad did not get the memo from the Supreme Court.

It is your job, should you choose to accept it, to inform them of your right to free speech. Speak out against the cowardly act of censorship! There is never an excuse for censorship. Stand up for your rights.

No censorship. Ever!

Glossary

Here is the vocabulary you need to say the worst possible things imaginable in the best way possible.

CENSORED is what you say when BLOCKED

CENSORED really means CLASSIFIED

CENSORED is a dirty word for BANNED

CENSORED instead of DENIED

CENSORED is a stronger way to say ACCESS DENIED

CENSORED usually replaces CONFIDENTIAL

CENSORED is a meaner WITHHELD

CENSORED is the worst possible FORBIDDEN

About the Damn Author

Jimmy Huston lives in Woodland Hills, California, where he is hiding out from the Methodist Church.

He has been researching this book for many years and is considered by many to be an expert on the subject of obscenity. That offends him greatly.

An avid procrastinator, his favorite hobbies are obfuscation, whimsy, and blasphemy.

Please don't tell his mother that he wrote this book.

www.byjimmyhuston.com
jh@byjimmyhuston.com

Reviews are usually appreciated.

Other Odd Books by Jimmy Huston

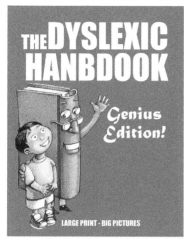

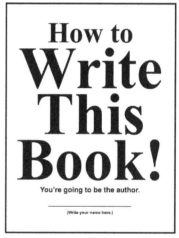

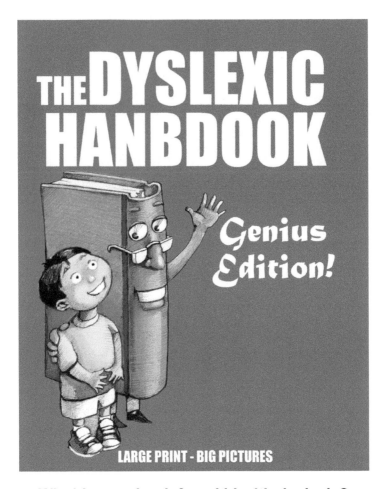

THE DYSLEXIC HANBDOOK

Genius Edition!

LARGE PRINT - BIG PICTURES

Who* buys a book for a kid with dyslexia?

Giving a self-help book to a dyslexic kid is like offering a drink of water to someone who is drowning.

So, have someone read it to you, so you can listen and think about it -- and look at the pictures.

This book is also available on Audible as an audiobook. (You'll have to imagine the pictures.)

* Someone who cares.

FIND IT WHEREVER GOOD BOOKS ARE DREADED

If you're reading this, you will not like this book. It's not for you.

This book is for the people who are *not* reading this.

They won't like it either, but it's short.

They'll like that.

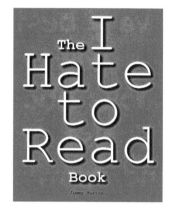

"I didn't actually read this book. If I had, I would have loved it — but I never will."
Billy

"Hate isn't a strong enough word for me. I loathe reading. I don't even like looking at pictures - which there are none of."
Wally

"This isn't what I wrote about this stupid book."
Zane

"This is an excellent coffee table book, if your coffee table hates to read."
Solomon

"This book made my teacher cry."
David

"My son loved this book. He said it was delicious."
Mr. Jones

"THIS BOOK IS SO DUMB THAT I COULD'VE WRITTEN IT."
Jimmy

www.i-hate-to-read.com

One of the very best new books about Christmas and reptiles!

Ripped from the headlines of Candy Cane Lane!

Follow little Nate-Nate as he explores Candy Cane Lane on Christmas Eve. He is not exactly welcomed by the neighborhood, but through his adventures Nate-Nate discovers the spirit of Christmas despite being a lowly snake in everyone's eyes.

When the joyful holiday mood is threatened, he slithers to the rescue and becomes the legend known far and wide as Nate-Nate the Christmas Snake.

No snakes were harmed in the writing of this book.

NOW AVAILABLE AS AN AUDIOBOOK FROM AUDIBLE.COM
Read by Sean Philip Glasgow

www.christmassnake.com

U-Draw books from Cosworth Publishing give kids a chance to add their own creatve artwork to these books.
www.udrawbooks.com

DEAD IS the NEW SICK

An Insiders Guide to Senility, Paranoia, and Curmudgery

"Warmly affectionate elder abuse."   — Methuselah

"Sadly funny..."
                              — Sophocles

"The Pet Rock of western literature."   — Anon.

"I don't feel so good."
                              — John Doe

Top 10 Warnings

1. Hospice is a crock. Keep a jug of water under the bed.
2. Write a will.
4. Hide it.
5. Don't walk toward the light.
6. Did you take your meds today today?
7. Are you sure?
8. What happened to #3?
9. Eat a pie.
10. If there has ever been something you wanted to do, but didn't for whatever reason, now is the time to do it! Start with this book!

Wisdom of the Aged

PG-65

Dead Is the New Sick

An Insider's Guide to Senility, Paranoia & Curmudgery

Jimmy Huston

Other Books from Cosworth Publishing
www.cosworthpublishing.com

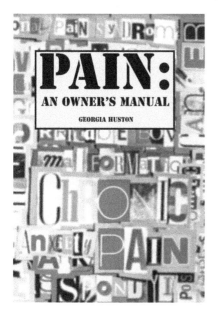

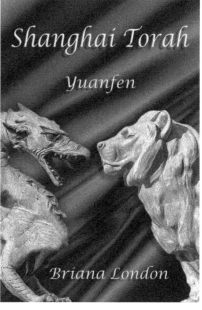